TOOLS FOR TEACHERS

- **ATOS:** 0.8
- **GRL:** C
- **WORD COUNT:** 28

- **CURRICULUM CONNECTIONS:** animals, habitats

Skills to Teach

- **HIGH-FREQUENCY WORDS:** a, has, in, it, look, out, the
- **CONTENT WORDS:** climbs, cub, fingers, forest, lives, mask, peeks, raccoon, striped, tail
- **PUNCTUATION:** exclamation points, periods
- **WORD STUDY:** long /a/, spelled ai (tail); long /e/, spelled ee (peeks); multisyllable words (fingers, forest, raccoon)
- **TEXT TYPE:** information report

Before Reading Activities

- Read the title and give a simple statement of the main idea.
- Have students "walk" though the book and talk about what they see in the pictures.
- Introduce new vocabulary by having students predict the first letter and locate the word in the text.
- Discuss any unfamiliar concepts that are in the text.

After Reading Activities

Ask the children to think about the environment that is the focus of the book. What do they think a forest is like? Invite them to discuss what makes a forest and then to name other animals and plants they think might live there.

Tadpole Books are published by Jump!, 5357 Penn Avenue South, Minneapolis, MN 55419, www.jumplibrary.com

Copyright ©2019 Jump. International copyright reserved in all countries. No part of this book may be reproduced in any form without written permission from the publisher.

Editor: Jenna Trnka **Designer:** Anna Peterson

Photo Credits: Sonsedska Yuliia/Shutterstock, cover, 6–7, 8–9, 16tr, 16br; Eric Isselee/Shutterstock, 1; Diana Carpenter/Shutterstock, 2–3, 16tm; Jeff Stamer/Shutterstock, 4–5, 16bm; Heiko Kiera/Shutterstock, 10–11, 16tl; Dssimages/Dreamstime, 12–13; jimkruger/iStock, 14–15 (foreground); Zack Frank/Shutterstock, 14–15 (background), 16bl.

Library of Congress Cataloging-in-Publication Data
Names: Nilsen, Genevieve, author.
Title: Raccoon cubs / by Genevieve Nilsen.
Description: (Tadpole edition) | Minneapolis, MN : Jump!, Inc., (2018) | Series: Forest babies
Identifiers: LCCN 2018007772 (print) | LCCN 2017061705 (ebook) | ISBN 9781624969720 (ebook) | ISBN 9781624969706 (hardcover : alk. paper) | ISBN 9781624969713 (pbk.)
Subjects: LCSH: Raccoon—Infancy—Juvenile literature.
Classification: LCC QL737.C26 (print) | LCC QL737.C26 N55 2018 (ebook) | DDC 599.76/321392—dc23
LC record available at https://lccn.loc.gov/2018007772

FOREST BABIES

RACCOON CUBS

by Genevieve Nilsen

TABLE OF CONTENTS

tadpole
books

RACCOON CUBS

Look! A raccoon cub!

tail

It has a striped tail.

mask

It has a mask.

finger

It has fingers.

It climbs.

It peeks out.

It lives in the forest.

WORDS TO KNOW

climbs

cub

fingers

forest

mask

tail

INDEX